Foreign Object

Foreign Object

Steven Teref

Negative Capability
PRESS
MOBILE, ALABAMA

TABLE OF CONTENTS

THE TUNNEL

PASSENGER

EMPTY SLEEVE: NOVICA TADIĆ

ACKNOWLEDGMENTS

"It lives and it disturbs, even crouched calmly in its depths."

– Vicente Huidobro

Dear Charles Simic

I live in your shadow.

I'm writing you a letter of endearment drunk with poetry, silence, and sadness from the death of Novica Tadić. Your original version of "White" stains me. I've written undergraduate papers about you. Dated you in my dreams. How do I break away? My forehead rests against the knob of a kitchen drawer. I want to tear you down yet I respect you. I'm now a foreign object survivor and write oblique prose poems about the blue blades of night. The ink of your influence indelibly shapes me. A masque of facile amusements drowns me. I hear the ring of garbage trucks.

Let's share a bottle of red wine.

With Reverence,
Steven Teref

SLAVIC SKIN

Sada Ovde

Among the hundred mole stars
a scar by her breast
marks the place from which
I've fallen, her skin
a negative of that other sky

I am the shadow fruit
she bites into
reminds her of that tearing
covering my body in Cyrillic I write:
сада овде – now here

Slavic skin. The little punishments gather. You may cut the hair of conquerors but you are still cut down by them. And when the village meets, you may not be thought of well. Broken sundials mark beauty's end and discovery's origin. Ask a question. I cannot answer. Again ask. Ask again. Until I cry. Dew gives spider webs in bushes a palatial glistening. Impalement opens the heart.

Belgrade

Veles carries the mother's name.
I am framed in her still throat.
One absence evolves into another
breach – this is my head, my hand.

Gypsy bane: sallow candles drip phlegm
on yellow petals. Beauty robbers
lend (   ) an inviting aesthetic.
Hooded crows on Novo Groblje stone.

Serbian Menu

Wither kidneys	120 din.
Young bull's sex glands and bowels	180 din.
Walnut crescents and coups	550 din.
Mushroom in many mournings	800 din.

Baba Yaga

Between the perfect knife and the honest flower, Baba Yaga's beach house emerges from the needle maze. Snow courses through her fickle veins as she sips coconut milk and cognac. She teases Moldovan girls from chat rooms into her cauldron.

Little Olga winces as she draws back the bandage from her right breast; her captivity sore hasn't healed since a man bit her.

Every girl's nerves unfurl in Baba Yaga's web. What hapless leap doesn't garner a few dinars? In the sun's inky afterglow, the dusky sea washes against Baba Yaga's bamboo door.

Holzerisms

Torture saves people from themselves.

Your oldest fears are your best friends.

Boredom begets sex.

Absolute honesty is a prison.

You are a victim of the rules you break.

Confession of an Orthodox Priest

St. Sava Temple: God's marble finger. Under the nail, the fungal underbelly of purgatory. The bones of St. Sava burn in concrete flames. Balkan shadows end in Cyrillic pools of toenail polish. The anonymous live with prayer scars for all the kneeling nights unanswered. I speak umber silence in a city ruled by a modern coconut deity and its discontents with creased sneakers, remainder books, fragrance-free masks. Cast-asides force the view of emaciated corpses rotting in tree branches, draped like drying bed sheets in the heat. The riverside villages along the Drina: bones strewn along iron mud banks. From pear branches, brandy bottles dangle like diamond earrings.

Translating Tadić (Version)

I open the door to my sister's room:
Novica Tadić cradles her small body
in his black embrace.

When translating you is done
I want you gone.

NIGHTMARIANS

Obstructivist

shock of sudden butterfly
holes from light arrive
ground overwhelms sky

every stain an insect
a blurring suicide tea
obstacle to beauty's bra
the unobtainable

flags, cities, a compulsive denial
if you can get around my wings
I am a wound worth devouring

Man Without Qualities

The Man Without Qualities never explored mating in the white forest tucked in God's garnet sleeve. Fraying sleep spores on the ram-motif kilim. The man's name fails to spring from within. He stands in his decadron glow and hiccups, as still in his mind as in the metal morning. Eyes are when a woman gazes. Water belongs to his anxiety, his waking. If he could drape himself in the graying. It's difficult for the man without. He waits for the elevator to the gun. From his imploding wax paper heart, from his seagull-stained windows, from the dead-end, from the long street, he hopes never to conceive.

Babysitter

If my head were shaved,
an encyclopedia of demons
would sprout: *Sitri*,
Bune, *Samigina*: the map
of my chthonian passage.

In the chase-with-a-carving-knife night,
in the handcuffed-to-the-bedpost day,
in the break-my-favorite-glass magic trick,
in the lick-my-crack-I'll-lick-yours bathroom,
he makes me wear red-and-black masks
to hide his curdled crave.

Give me an Irish wolfhound
so the babysitter can go home
to his candied grave.

Wanderer

for Ronald Sparkes

The wanderer of the mudflats pads across the peat moss. Hallowed legs haunt him. The cleaver in him. Ironworks. The sun-brushed memory. A maggot school. The suture from the Whipple runs across his abdomen like a brown grimace. Parched eyes. Sparkhood quarters the stars.

Where are
the fluorescent flicker docks,
the bookie dim bars,
drunks earthed in talk?
All erred early in jars.

Geraldine

night　　　　　　　gave

owl　　　　　　　gnarled

Are shadows not

creeping　　　　　meat

field　　　　　　　folly

..

　　　　　　　　　roots

curdled　　　　　eyes

jealous wings?

　　　　　　　　renounce

autumn　　　　　diction

..

　　　　　　　　　dim

wart　　　　　　　tongue

Do they not rush

fragrant

weakened　　　　face

..

castle

musty   sleep

     to smother flight?

wraith   chain

emerald   shout

    . .

insect   lace

        lash

    Does gravel canvas

flesh   hearth

        descends

    . .

overcast

limp   prison

    both prayer and eye?

slithers   over

leoline   slumber

Watchmakers

the bittersweet carriage in Paris

    organ of excess
    round-bottomed with sanctity

sense 'failure'

    enforce it
    let it be tender

as thermal resins

    crack wood bodies
    across a lower pose

close, fine, sable

    strokes on a fiddle
    set to quiver

dismissive noise

    with patience
    wandering

To the Holy Ghost

You fashion faith from void. The hatred without within awaiting virgin birth. I can't sing. My broken throat rasps. You embody the history of prayer and forgiveness, you carny catalytic converter. How else could Christ be moved to transmogrify me from an auto mechanic's sponge into a gold chalice cradling holy blood? I'm afraid of the distance. Either you create God or you leave town.

Silence of the Scales

At Nero's cookout, pluck a lyre on a skull mattress to the pulse of flame. Pawn false teeth in the defoliated night swamp. Glue barracuda teeth inside the crabmeat house. Before the neck gleam, the cold window:

> *In sleep, Nero wailed down the halls of the Domus Aurea.*
> *He cracked his whip. He weighed his harrow:*
> *Was he a patient or collector of fever?*

> *He listened for any sign within.*

Son

Between scalers and curettes, the oblivion porno moistens his canines.

Grace

A silence that heals and destroys in equal measure.

Father

This item is currently unavailable.

THE TUNNEL

1

Start a hole. Enter unpainted and common.
Tunnel in red and timorous. What will it reveal?
The tunnel is subject to what the eyes fill it with.

The air is warm and close, bright
with phosphorescent lichen.
Dirt and rock absorb your sweet breath.

Old made fresh through new eyes.
What appears to be white feathered wolves
huddle up ahead. They feed on what appears

to be caterpillars clinging to dangling roots,
snatch slow flies from the air, then scatter.
Follow them.

2

Earth gives way to descending rock.
Guided by lichen the tunnel widens
to tombs and thorn temples.

A thronging mass of wolf-like ash keepers,
paper asps and mad-daubed
greet you.

Cast in division,
you vie for the deepest shadows
grown in rocky recesses.

No separate sound
for sacred. How will you adapt?
What new year could bend you to their rituals?

Advance far toward thorn temple as into
soothe region. You are the tribute, a line
that reaches from thorn, west to.

3

Ash keepers shiver in spring-hover.
Thorn temples contain perfumed ashes,
urned in mad-daubed husks.

Your conversion happens there.
Your misspent life redeemed there.
You once said sometimes love is not enough.

That sometimes brought you here.
The amount of pain a pan will hold.
The tunnel receives all

that have given up on scarring,
on breakage; when the corners get too tight –
dig. You are here: to witness.

Catch a keeper by the head.
Won't hurt you—beyond that now.
Wipe away with your thumbs

the whitish film that covers
its half-healed canker eyes.
The shrunken orbs rove sightless.

What makes keepers tunnel through their winter,
to seek further hollows, further divisiveness?
Their westering will never reach east.

4

Emerge from your hiding.
Mad-daubed can do no harm.
What flowers could you seek

in the overwintering of tunnels?
What drill could end this?
You remember how rain

struck nocturnal wood
but that can't happen here.
Dust litters the tunnels.

How you wish you could
fill the tunnels with rain
and feel the comfort of wood.

Gaze down a tunnel, its black mouth.
Fill the opening with howl
and verge through thin cope.

5

Draped on ladders, paper asps seem harmless.
You have doubts. They are mal – can sting.
Do not look. Their fierce looks.

You cannot chrysalis.
You cannot claw.
Sleep will not find you.

You have desired to be impaled
by falling stalactites. You have desired
to throw yourself upon a stalagmite.

You cannot chrysalis.
You cannot cling.
Sleep will not overtake you.

Asps come emitting a crumbled
sound from their undulating stingers. The slow
crinkle of their skin over rocks.

6

Notches on your arm mark what may be days.
What is a day? A year? A lifetime?
How long have you been crawling

around in tunnels? You feed on larvae.
Wax moths fan their wings
and guard the entrance to thorn temples,

the rituals, the illusion
of ascension. Re-enforcing
how the sky lies, how ladders lead nowhere.

Wings stroke the minutes.
Their buzz resonates
in the walls. You chew through the wall.

7

You're trapped in a storage room filled with detritus
of dead keepers, shed larval skins, wax caps.
Attracted by the scent, beetles and moths

wiggle from under the door. Your bare feet
can't crush them all. Listen to the noise
from other rooms, of witnesses.

In the frenzy, you need escape.
If not, you will melt and flow
down through the walls. Stains

are never removed. How could they be replaced?
Like wax moths, they persist for years. The dead
attract beetles. Keep moving and close up

your honey-head. Enter through another hole
you found loosely caulked. Your vain
attempts to prevent further stings.

8

You succumb to the honeyed venom
of asps rising from the vale. They have come
to make a moist tent of your body.

Pinned down, you inspire a loose creation
that inhabits your lament. Their mission
is to drag you to the river of remembering.

They are lured by your slur, hiss, and lust;
your softening tissue, the facile flow
from other mountings, the shrine

of your body serrated. This venom
injects gradations of despair. You are caught
between vesper and asp.

The lance's barbed meaning hooks into you,
longs for your edges. Barbs anchor into your flesh.
You are an unlit altar

clawed by a deeper wound.
Stained lace covers your abdomen. Vesper through
your poisoned canal, between wounds.

Asps sting your liar process, your lockout,
your silence and motel sanctuaries.
Your vesper unable to rip through

wound's persistence, the firmness
of your flesh. The comfort of strangers
haunts you even in death. This is a realm

where even roaming fails you.
Where else would you go
without this place to be imagined by you?

THE FOREIGN OBJECT

30

I have reached halfway
give or take a decade

I hear the tug-of-war
played at night
their thick shoulders bump into the walls

it is not the house that shifts & settles
it has all day for that

my time creaks
keeping me awake
when I try to sleep

Event Poem

"your wolf will have become another wolf, your sister a different sister"
– Italo Calvino

Folktale:

The dream-wolf bears its fangs:
ghost proteins through glass veins

umbilicaled to ground, the child
waits her turn. The sibling wolf

slavers over his sister.
Their parental eye: the void.

Creation myth:

From the first blood drop, a ladybug fluttered;
a red bell pepper sprouted from the second;
from the third, a fox.

Fox hunt:

Squandered breath,
veins' blue tracks,
fiery train of dawn.

Remains:

Fox skull: a field mouse
scuttles from socket to socket.

Running To

teeth are no barrier
to a body obsolete in its curves

unwinds about her
obvolute passages of shadow
ladyslips, bound to eye's confessions

sleep and urine rationed out
into dry dream-mouth

stars' silver nails: malice
indigo ravine
mauve reach, swollen distance

Instinct. This is my hand.
These are my hands.
This is my head. Tears, days die under my nails.
My lungs, my fun bread brain and kidneys crawl.
Seek your eyes on my body.
In testicles. Intestines. This is all I know.
This will take me to hell in a chrome thunder cart.

Stiff Flames

His smile reaches only so far across his face. He makes bank transactions at night. He wears a thick veil. His story on his cheek, it blasts his future. He couldn't stop drinking for more than four months. Hated himself. Lit himself on fire in an abandoned concrete bunker by the railroad tracks. The smoke rising from his isolated body attracted unwanted help. The want ad for sobriety answered in an oxygen tent. He wears the mask of his past. Mirrors reflect shame. Does he place the importance of one error over another? He won't answer. The charred husk of night surrounds him. It has expended its use. He found comfort in neither heat nor cold. Under the cloak of his room, smothered by memory. He dreams of stiff flames:

midnight noose

tanning
    hate

                       agile
                            years
      flare
              in
          detox tents

        sand maps
 of mirrors

    deflect
      denial

   charred
    comfort

Night letter. Black dogs hang out windows again;
eat air. Gloom guarded within.
"No roses, only leaves that burn." How you've come
to speak of your favorite flower. I know the self that drinks
when nerve-heavy, gallowed-breath. An arm crawls to cigarettes.
vodka eclipses cup, styrofoams the mind.

Each night letter sets fire to its own starling
and dances a black dare around it
until the starling burns out.

Left in sweat. Blood shapes stones that immure us.
You show me breasts past suckling.
Number me among your lovers; run fingers
along my fault-lines. When you die—blanketed.
Ending the labyrinth, the fingerprints.

Unlit bodies.   On your lap in the unlit
                             bedroom, recounted
the secrets of your body. In the tub, baptized
between wet breasts. No longer your son.

Room with ocean.   The ocean bursts through bedroom glass.
                          Paper seagulls sway from a hanging mobile.
An empty crib bobs between us.

                    Mother, we are going to drown.

Water crushes with a nursery rhyme:

        two people in a wet room / swept away by Neptune's broom

                    Seaweed cocoons
                    and gives us fins.

Sibling tide.   Departure aspect: dive whitened
                                     into the shadow portrait.

    Seaweed mother is dead.

                                Sister, choke on kelp cords.

Black waves stretch against the shore.
Whiter fingers tap against sand, await
your arrival.

Salt machine.   I envy the grace of the wheel
                  with a barnacled back. Fish bones
fill my lungs. My bladder houses a sea urchin. All my angles
caught on coral. Behind the waves hands splash.
There's more to oceans than Neptune's bullying.

In costume.   Snow harvesters maintain their grace
                    in spring. Icy water pours
from their navels. Silhouette's process into snakehead. Into air.
The imperfection of white. Flaw's jubilant blue. Sweepers usher
in sunrise. And what to do with the mouth? A finger enters
or a tongue. Eyes unlock. There you are
lounging against the retina. Applaud.

Water from Hands

the earth's
arthritic pirouettes
slow
in aimless theater

    aura machines
             in scroll burnout

    static snow
        over green
            gravity

etymology of meat
where possibilities end

bravery descends by ankle

a body
between falling
rasputinously
dies

a flood inherent

a waking burn
in glass

girl gets out of bed grown up
boy checks his watch: noon

Found Letter 1

My house is closed.
I don't have any kiss –
you can come.

Found Letter 2

I have no light.
My hitting is not working.
My man door is not closing.

Fertility

In the centigrey light of the living room, a skinned gutted deer dangles by calves on meat hooks. From the cavity, 500,000 cockroaches scuttle up its legs and across the ceiling. Eyelashes of ex-lovers tremble in the crevices of crown molding. In the dim kitchenette, add a charred corpse effect before the lesion throbs and stretches in the cold stove.

Gaps

The ocean chafes the shore; fog closes gaps in the air. The grit of time departs the red Sognefjord boathouse. What the innocence manager appreciates when children play in the bird pool: the hour the birds flee into the infinite. Flee the peninsula, the June sky, the approaching storm. Pack the curse.

Foreign Object

I spill earth in your name.

I wait in your emerald. Cisplatin's turbine obscures October's rustle. I can't jump off the horror-go-round. The blood marker stock market. Behind my cornea: a wind-wrapped flight. Vitreous fluid: ghost station dust. Airplanes born in fiery buildings. Inside fear: x-ray light.

   None so large as —

the white orb blurs,
then closes,

                   but no,
                     not *closed*. My body rapt.
                Not *catheter*, hostile though;
                    nor *cantaloupe*. A crab,
               clamping; open and fold.

For Julie

Loss, the egg,
casts lives through
candling

Not quite missing——
not quite
the body

Yearning cracks
the cast
iron shell

*

At the end of the pier
night blots out
the lake

*

Memory whittles
the soft
focus

Scratches time——
scrapes the play——
the part

Yet shivs
the hollow——
the heart

Names Disappear

Dawn deals not light—

I am but a knot of neurons
laboring on the mattress
a mother lost
a father bereft

figments have no weight
the aftertaste of love and lust
yet phantoms hold court—
their sated dust

a hand is but sand
a path to disappoint

my hand held mother's eyes
closed—could not deny
father's from seeing
me

the topaz in his pancreas
housed regret for the son lost

the son housed a loss
between his legs

the bitter that binds
found in the node
the foreign object

*

Dawn rises not to cast sight—

in our midst shades toss
their fading touch

the earth mines and mints
minds us till we withdraw
into its mindless maw

a name is a wisp of sound
echoing for a few ears
before the ground balks

mutes the strained tongue
that lunges to imprint
a moist pause

Crow Waves

Answers trickle from a salivary gland. Acoustic tumors in the cheek squeak like patent leather shoes of the conspiracy theorist. The smoking petrol fields on the horizon are the barrier, the roof that sheathes me from the sun. The long wrecks of sleep wrap me in shadows. I'm not the uncirculated coin in the hand but the shucked oyster in the radiation field. I'm without walls. I live in the leakage. Cooked white rat flesh in a cold oven. Am I an integrated body? A bullet in the eye. Brains swept under the IEDs. Meth-heads roam rehab halls. Crows startle in heavy light.

Vaulted. Glassed night
beckons
for light. Humor it
with candles; break it with spotlight
hammers.

Descent. *Spining* memory, pining
for sun. My garnet brain,
a calcium-weaver renetting remembrance.
Fat fruit flies burst like pomegranate seeds.

At the end.   Rose-hatch: blue shadows of pubescence. Eyes
                    stir sunset into blown glass wonder:
echo sea of bats, lark flight, rabbits bounding over uncut grass. Fireflies.

Etrog. Beauty in pockmarks and cellulite. The willow in one another. Skate on the half-frozen brook. Only commas separate the days. Perfection resides in bruises.

Sand.   Sunrise, a widening aperture.
               Eyes on a dimmer.
Tangible behind glass, the street rewrites the meek.

The sand bridge divides me.

Mail didn't come today.

Landing pads.   Fruit fly on a sea green wall. Still life in pale streaks.
                Vents let the airplanes in. The long rattle engine waits
for the trap door spider
                to sprout
                        garnet wings.

Body Bag

How papery pleasure is – the genuine forms nobody.

A Walk in Mausoleum Row

A squirrel black bounds up an old oak.
This land of unquenched night, its tombs
like gated thorns on purpled grass.
White addresses, jealous mothers,
covet the dead in wintry wombs.
Round the columbarium, geese
gather; beaks to ground – clean shadows.

Murder

Beloved winged-ravagers
catch air, sweep
off cliffs to rocky
shore; ashes
from a funeral urn –
mountainous night
cast down.

A Body

near the window, near the lake
a body can enter either
look at it, enough
it's there, eyes
can see the openness
paint a room
minus a door

PASSENGER

(PASSENGER and RIDER sit next to each other.
PASSENGER pulls a silver pocket watch in her mouth.
The pieces glisten with saliva.)

PASSENGER

I marshal the word's kernel woundings.

(The sound of dry wings, as of a large beetle, beat the air. A
shadow flutters behind PASSENGER.)

RIDER

Rat memory is immortal.
    A rat traces its route
    along a wall.
    When the wall is removed
    the rat will scuttle along
    the same route
    as if the wall remained.

(Pause.)

RIDER

I'm wound in the same stained sheet.

PASSENGER

The human mouth divides in the evening, just after nightfall.
    Claustrophobic behind the curtain,
it ponders fright the violent light the one mutiny;
orgasms divide the night
but are unable to disable clocks
in prison cells. Clock, cell,
and word – fixed in their triad.

RIDER

Cold plans not drawn from lesser hands
roll up on the blue drafting board;
frost falls across Icarusian zones.
Light drops to ground like pebbles.
Tunnels encase my shame.

(PASSENGER makes a grotesque face.)

RIDER

The rodent-run brain
    defined by ignorance

more than knowledge.
I structure ignorance
like a beaver building
a dam. I flood one land
while another lies parched.
How can I arrive
at a stop unnamed?

(PASSENGER sucks on the pocket watch.)

RIDER

I kissed my mother's desiccated hand.
My inborn betrayal burned it. I can't divide myself
from the word. I can't divine
the monochrome décor of the void.

PASSENGER

Who knows the title?
Until the mouth—
You know what takes place here.
It is all plasma and black imagination.
The crypt in the eye.

RIDER

The shudder in mother......her face surrounded by child...
caressed her cold cheek......sorry...my camera seemed to be the first
time..........had her face......beyond the actual here...escaped a sec-
ond.........desired to possess her face...kept her.........my body a
camera......kept pressing the shutter............desired her face...the
first to have her......camera kept the shudder...her cold cheek kept...

(Pause.)

RIDER

Why do voices
nest in the vast?

PASSENGER

The Museum of Lost Objects.
The vignettes of loneliness found in
discarded ledgers, water-logged paperbacks
with faded spines, a tin cupping assorted buttons,
cracked Christmas ornaments,
lost letters from torn lovers,
bent bicycle wheels, frayed shoe laces,

and 1147 beads of orbiting space junk.

(Pause.)

RIDER

I scoop found prayers
        from plastic beads.

PASSENGER

Prayers: the spines
        of insecure kingdoms.
        Repayment to the dead
        after you rub your cock
        against un-giving breasts
        of granite angels.

(PASSENGER wags her obscene tongue.)

RIDER

What currency
        does silence accept?

PASSENGER

The charity of a red giant.

(Pause.)

PASSENGER

What art will outlast man?

RIDER

Stonehenge.

PASSENGER

What art will outlast man?

RIDER

A heron rookery.

PASSENGER

What art will outlast man?

RIDER

Twinkies.

PASSENGER

What art will outlast man?

RIDER

Dick Clark's collagen death mask.

PASSENGER

The answer sleeps behind a wax seal.

(PASSENGER gnashes her teeth.)

(Pause.)

RIDER

When I wake from anesthesia
  I regain the words of a child.

PASSENGER

God forgives, but dogs don't.
  The grudge of canines corrupts films
  with rabid silken lips.

RIDER

All comes down to word-grace;
  how to accept
  losing, luck, and light.

PASSENGER

Despair toothpicks your smile.
  You whimper and wake at 3 a.m.
  You write outlines to novels you'll never finish
  to stave off your fear of erasure.

(Pause.)

RIDER
(shouts to the panicked rhythm of claustrophobia)
THE SUBWAY |
  A PRISON | THE WORD | |
  THE PRISON | IMMORTAL | AND BROKEN |
  | THE WORD | FIXED | AND FINITE | |
  I | THE RAT |
  BRIGHT ENDGAME

| BLACK | MALFORMED | MOIRA | MOUTH |
    | | |
THE PASSENGER | | VICTOR | AGLARE
|
THE WORD | | DESPAIR | |
I | THE RAT | | ENDGAME | THE WORD |
THE WINDING | DEEP | THROUGH | THE WORD
| | FIXES | ME | |
A NAIL | THE WORD | | CRIPPLED | WITHIN |
THE MOUTH | A BIN | I BREATHE | |
(*an inching intake of air*) | |
PASSENGER | THE WARDEN |
THE EYE | ENGULFS | THE LUMINESCENT RAT |
| THE LABYRINTH | WORDS |
CAMERAS | RECORD | CLOCKS | CLOCKS |
CLOCKS | GOUGE | THE WALLS | |
|
THE RIDER | ALLOTTED | A WINDOW |
    | THE WINDOW | CONCEALED | | |
| |
THE WAX | KEYHOLE
| PERFUME | SET | ALIGHT | |
 FURNITURE | AFLOAT | IN ROOMS | IN FUMES |
    | (*a gasping for air*) | |
THE SHADOW | SEWN IN | PERFORMANCE |
    |
PASSENGER | | ENTROPIC | ARCHITECT |
   | | THE PASSENGER | IN EACH | BODY
|
THE WARDEN | PERPETUAL | WEIGHT |
THE WIGHT | WITHIN | THE HUNGRY | PUPIL |
ABSORBS | A BODY | |
| BLACK | CELLS | IN EVERY | ANATOMY | |
THE NULLING | JUDGE | SNUFFS | THE TUNNEL.

(A distasteful expression crosses PASSENGER's face.
She pulls a hair from her mouth.)

PASSENGER

You tried to burn me out of you
    when I have survived the burning of Troy,
    the burning of Rome,
    the Great Chicago Fire,
    spontaneous combustion,
    the burning of widows and witches.
Ah, the gleam from bride-burning.
The flames that funneled through Joan of Arc's body;
the smolder of unrequited love,
the ovens of Auschwitz.
Reborn at Trinity,
      I thrived in Hiroshima and Nagasaki.
Stravinsky composed a ballet in my name.
I am the burning monk;
the mute
    encircle my shrunken
    charred head.
My heart doesn't burn.
I survive in a glass chalice.
    (pause)
I will outlast the enthusiasm of hope.
I will outlast the death of the Sun.
    (chuckles)
You want to drown me?
    (PASSENGER slobbers on the pocket watch.
    She delicately swings her moist watch in front of RIDER's
    face as if she intends to hypnotize RIDER, snatches it, then
    places the watch in RIDER's shirt pocket with a gentle pat.
    She leans close to RIDER's ear.)
I can swim. Can you?

    (CURTAIN)

EMPTY SLEEVE: NOVICA TADIĆ

Hands Full

You're here. You've arrived.
You're here. Everywhere
you have your hands
full.

You tear, cut,
and release
trapped shrieks.

You are the Mistress.
You're busy.
You cast a black
shroud
over the world.

I Dream of Being Buried

I dream of being buried.
The dirt eats my limbs
and nose.

The people I used to know
turn their heads
and depart.

The procession disperses,
cars roar
overcrowded with junk
and wicked
mocking children.

After a Brief Illness

After a brief yet serious
illness, he wrote verse
fiery and senseless.

He watched and read.
Read, watched, groaned.
Beyond belief,
he invited his neighbors.

Neighbors, being neighbors,
sit and help themselves.

As usual, they stare
vacantly at poetry.
A poem is a black growth.

Like a Warlock

Like a warlock averse to light,
I shun the town square on clear days
where crowds gather.

I hug the walls, tree rows, and shadows;
benches dot the boulevard.

I watch the furies clash,
and yet, I don't know who's what
nor what banners they're waving.

Still, sometimes, on a hot summer afternoon,
I'm a vampire chasing his own shadow.

Raven

While fast asleep
in an empty train compartment
someone snuck in
and searched my pockets.

Since he found only
newspaper clippings
and crumpled scraps of paper,
he rifled through them
and on one wrote:

"Next time, if I don't find any loot,
I'll rip out your liver."

Empty Sleeve, Dream

As I lie in a dream,
you slip your empty
black sleeve
    over me
sew it up and carry
  me down the stairs
into the night.

Acknowledgments

I wish to thank Paul Hoover, Clayton Eshleman, Arielle Greenberg, Suzanne Buffam, and the editors who have supported my work.

The following poems have appeared in these journals:

Action Yes: "Babysitter" and "Event Poem"
Apocryphal Text: Special Issue: "The Tunnel"
Arsenic Lobster: "Night Letter" (Pushcart Prize nomination)
Black Clock: "Slavic Skin"
Columbia Poetry Review: "Stiff Flames," "Water from Hands," "Running To," "The Obstructivist," "Salt Machine," and "In Costume"
Court Green: "Found Letter" (1)
Dirty Goat: "Translating Tadić," "Hands Full," "I Dream of Being Buried," "Like a Warlock," and "Raven"
Masque & Spectacle: "Fertility," "Foreign Object," and "Crow Waves"
Negative Capability Press' *Thirty-Three: An[niversary] Anthology*: "Confession of an Orthodox Priest," and "To the Holy Ghost"
Red Shoes Revisited: "Geraldine"
Rhino: "Man Without Qualities"
Ricochet Review: "Room with Ocean"
Samizdat: "30" and "*Sada Ovde*"
scissors and spackle: "Wanderer" and "Gaps"
Xpressions: "Watchmakers"

Versions of "Body Bag," "A Walk in Mausoleum Row," "Murder," and "A Body" appeared in the chapbook *Dust* (Ignavia Press).

Versions of "Instinct" previously appeared in a collaborative sound piece of the same name with Steve Barsotti, and in *The Bongo Lesson* by performance art group Phoenixworm.

"Passenger" was performed by Jassira Vardak and Steven Teref for the Red Rover Series on March 16, 2013.

"Night Letter" republished in *Arsenic Lobster 2010 Anthology*.

The Novica Tadić translations were co-translated from the Serbian with Maja Teref.

In "Geraldine," "are shadows not" is appropriated from James Shirley's "Death the Leveller" and "jealous wings" is taken from John Milton's "L'Allergro." "Found Poem 1" and "Found Poem 2" are appropriated from student responses to a writing prompt on the BEST Literacy Test.

www.ingramcontent.com/pod-product-compliance
Lightning Source LLC
Chambersburg PA
CBHW062112090426
42741CB00016B/3400